I0156852

God's Hitman

*I'll Make You an Offer
You Can't Refuse!*

Richard Mayfield

TEACH Services, Inc.
P U B L I S H I N G
www.TEACHServices.com • (800) 367-1844

World rights reserved. This book or any portion thereof may not be copied or reproduced in any form or manner whatever, except as provided by law, without the written permission of the publisher, except by a reviewer who may quote brief passages in a review.

The author assumes full responsibility for the accuracy of all facts and quotations as cited in this book. The opinions expressed in this book are the author's personal views and interpretations, and do not necessarily reflect those of the publisher.

This book is provided with the understanding that the publisher is not engaged in giving spiritual, legal, medical, or other professional advice. If authoritative advice is needed, the reader should seek the counsel of a competent professional.

Copyright © 2020 Richard Mayfield

Copyright © 2020 TEACH Services, Inc.

ISBN-13: 978-1-4796-1204-8 (Paperback)

ISBN-13: 978-1-4796-1205-5 (ePub)

Library of Congress Control Number: 2020909928

Texts credited to NKJV are taken from the New King James Version®. Copyright ©1982 by Thomas Nelson, Inc. Used by permission. All rights reserved.

TEACH Services, Inc.
PUBLISHING
www.TEACHServices.com • (800) 367-1844

Table of Contents

Introduction

I never opened God's Instruction Book until I was seventy-two years old and sentenced to five years in the Colorado state prison system. This got my attention, since a five year stretch at my age appeared like a life sentence and it was very possible that I could die in prison. One thing that's easy to acquire in prison is the Holy Bible. However, my very first introduction to "THE KEYS TO THE KINGDOM" was presented to me December 30, 1951, by the Intermediate Sunday School Department of Grace Methodist Church in Rochester, New York, when I was only twelve years old. I know how exact this appears; however, I still possess this same Holy Bible (King James Version). HIS Word will never pass away!

What follows is my personal testimony of what it was like, what happened, and what it's like now.

In the Beginning

Why would a man leave his warm home
on Christmas Eve to drive seventeen
miles in the snow?

When I came to the end of my rope, I was completely exhausted and worn out from pretending. Finally—ultimately—I surrendered it all. Though I didn't know it at the time, this would become the best day of my life.

Looking into the mirror as I sat at the bar ordering my third martini, I experienced what might be called my "moment of truth." For the first time, I was convinced I no longer wanted to go home to my family drunk anymore. I paid for my martini, guzzled it down, and left the bar.

I didn't know what to do or where to go. I lived in Loveland, Colorado, but that day I was drinking in Greeley, about twenty miles away. So I decided to drive to nearby Fort Collins to find out if I could get help for my drinking problem. I had heard about AA and I knew I could probably find their phone number in the telephone directory. I located the numbers in the phone book. I dialed and a man answered.

"Blacker's Radiator Shop," he said. I nervously told him that I must have dialed the wrong number.

"What are you looking for?" he replied. I told him I was trying to contact AA.

I admitted for the first time in my life that I had a drinking problem and I needed help

---

"You've got the right place," he said. We talked and I admitted for the first time in my life that I had a drinking problem and I needed help. The man invited me to his place of business and gave me directions to get there.

After I got to his shop, he locked the door and flipped the "Open" sign over to "Closed." I wondered what I had walked into. He introduced himself as "RB" and looked me square in the eye and said, "How can I help you?"

"I can't quit drinking on my own," I replied. RB sat down and shared his experience, strength and hope with me. He described his association with AA and told me that he had not had a drink in quite a few days. He said he owed his sobriety to AA.

After we talked awhile, he said there were four other men that I should probably get to know if I "was serious about doing something about my drinking." The men's names were Harry, Ken, Rudy, and Woody. I shook RB's hand and set out to find Harry.

I ended up spending the afternoon with Harry, Ken, Rudy, and Woody. They shared their stories with me so I might be better able to decide if I wanted what they had—if the outcome would be worth the great effort involved.

Here's what I remember most: These five men stopped everything they were doing that December afternoon to try to help someone they had never met before. They cared. And their caring was something I would come to understand—but not that day. This instant friendship with these men was the beginning of my sobriety.

Woody, in particular, took me under his wing. I began to see him every morning for coffee in his little locksmith shop behind his home. I sat in my car every morning waiting for him to come out to open up his place of business, Woody's Lock and Key.

He never once appeared to get irritated or tired of my ranting and confused babbling, my grandiose ideas of worldly wealth and success. I had no idea he had had plenty of experience listening to other

---

I'm sure he thought I would not show up. Drunks like me very seldom tell the truth. But I kept my word

---

drunks. He always impressed me by saying that he had sobriety through AA *one day at a time*. He said that even though he had the price of a bottle of whiskey in his pocket he no longer wanted it. The craving and terrible obsession for alcohol had been lifted. I certainly wanted what Woody had.

The next meeting of AA in this area was three days away on Christmas Eve, back home in Loveland, which was seventeen miles south of Fort Collins. Woody was insistent about taking me to this meeting— if I was willing to go. I was very willing and yet, for some reason, I told Woody I would meet him there. We bantered back and forth for some time before Woody finally consented to meet me at the eight o'clock meeting. I'm sure he thought I would not show up. Drunks like me very seldom tell the truth. But I kept my word.

It was snowing as I walked up the steps and entered the meeting hall for my very first AA meeting. As I entered the room, I immediately saw Woody and felt relieved that I knew at least one person.

I couldn't understand why this beautiful little man would leave his family in Fort Collins on a snowy Christmas Eve and drive seventeen miles in the dark to a meeting to see if this person he knew nothing about would actually show up to the AA meeting. I didn't know it that day, but I had had my last drink.

Several years would pass before I understood the depth of caring of Woody and other people in AA. This understanding happened when Woody died. I was new and still too selfish and self-centered to attend his funeral. I owed so much to this man and others in AA, yet I did not attend his funeral.

Much later, the day finally arrived when I would kneel at Woody's grave with tears in my eyes. I made my amends. I apologized from the depths of my soul for not saying goodbye.

I'll never forget that December afternoon Woody took me aside and talked to me. This is how sobriety begins, and how AA continues to work, by one alcoholic talking to another. Woody had unselfishly helped me to freedom.

Robin W., Marty B., and Me

Robin Williams was a superstar. As a comedian, actor, improviser, and person extraordinaire he was indeed amazing. He was loved and sought after by millions. So what happened? What went so wrong? He had fame, personal awards, wealth, accolades, respect, and was loved by all, so what happened that would cause Robin to end his life so sadly? We can contemplate, speculate, intellectually analyze, and even guess with a shot in the dark what might have went wrong.

So what qualifies me to address anyone on this subject? Nothing really! I assure everyone I will never be an expert in anything except my own story. In the story of Marty and me, Marty was my very best friend up until the time he took his own life. I was so angry! I decided I would not attend

Marty's funeral. I would not pay any respect to his final act, which I really thought he didn't deserve. I was initially just not able to accept death by suicide.

Three days prior to Marty's suicide some of the men from our group came to me stating they felt Marty was in danger of doing something foolish or even life-threatening and that I should go and try to reason with him not to do anything "stupid." My response to them was, "Don't worry about Marty; he'll be okay." Three days later Marty cut his wrists and bled to death and I selfishly was very angry and hurt. I had absolutely no right or reason to react this way but, nevertheless, I did.

Marty and I were very much alike and had a great deal in common. We each had ten years clean and sober in a twelve-step recovery program. We each had more than one moment when we thought we were pretty hot stuff in the program and others would do well to follow our lead. How vain is that? Don't get me wrong—I loved Marty, still do, and always will, but he's been gone now for over thirty years and I'm still here. So how did that happen when we were so much alike?

The day of Marty's funeral I woke up from a sound sleep at 3 AM, asking myself what right did I have not to go to his funeral? The truth was, I didn't have any right, and I realized I wanted to go to Marty's final celebration to praise him and pay my final respects to my best friend. I needed to do this for who he was and what he had become—and not for what he finally did. I was to celebrate Marty's life, not his death. I came to praise him … not to bury him. While attending the funeral I realized for the first time in my life if I would search diligently within myself, I might be permitted to understand how all this could happen.

As I look back on the time I had with Marty, I appreciate the fact that we spent a few moments every day with each other. We would share our experience, strength, and our understanding of the written program with each other and anyone else who had a need and a desire to know more. One of the things I remember most about Marty was his gift of persuasion. He knew better than most that his personal guarantee of sobriety was dependent upon his unselfish concern for the welfare of others who desperately wanted freedom from the vice-like grip of alcohol addiction. I personally witnessed Marty many times in action, convincing some new prospect to attend a meeting with him to acquire this newfound freedom from "King Alcohol." For his own sobriety he knew that helping others worked when everything else in his life would fail. He could create the idea in anyone that they could get well if they would simply surrender to God and clean up their own

---

Complete surrender is not the problem; it is our resistance to the problem that ultimately causes our destruction

---

backyard. Yet Marty knew that his own sobriety was precarious so long as he placed his independence on anyone or anything ahead of his dependence upon the power of the universe which he knew was God. We were aware that we knew only a little and yet our ego would shout to the world that we knew all. How vain of us!

I honestly believe that his separation from his Heavenly Father was the root cause of his downfall. It is the foundational problem of our own making. Complete surrender is not the problem; it is our resistance to the problem that ultimately causes our destruction. Clearly it simply is our own free will. Searching diligently within myself I was permitted to finally understand it's not about me, it's not about Marty, it's not about anyone, but rather it's all about God. We are all God's kids and that's really it—there is no other answer. "After all, our problems were of our own making. Bottles were only a symbol. Besides, we have to stop fighting anybody or anything. We have to!" Again, the *Big Book* rings true. We must surrender to win. Marty was a master at helping other people relate to him and yet he tragically ended his own life without surrendering to the one true relationship available with his Father. Absolutely nothing is availed with half measures.

My final act, unlike Marty's, began by being convicted of theft and sentenced to five years in prison at Four Mile Correctional Facility in Canyon City, Colorado. I entered prison at seventy-two years old with thirty-eight years of continuous sobriety in Alcoholics Anonymous behind me, and I wanted to die. This was not the first time I thought about committing suicide, which now looked like a step up from where I was. God however, had a different plan for my life. I was to meet a man named Adam, who was the most spiritual person I had ever met, and it was he who introduced me to Jesus Christ. He was not only gentle and concerned, he was blessed with great understanding and superior intelligence. Needless to say, he was the most remarkable person I had ever known. God introduced, Adam led, and I followed. To this day I'm alive, confident, and at peace with God much of the time. So what happened? I finally surrendered my life to God. Sure, I knew about God, but there is a difference in knowing about and truly *knowing Him*. This was the solution that I had looked for all my life and with God's infinite wisdom I was to find it in Four Mile Prison. I served time with Jesus Christ and what better way to avert death and misery than to ultimately find Him and His twelve followers.

I had to cry before I could laugh; I had to die before I could live; I had to surrender to win; and now I must give it away to keep it. So now why did Robin Williams and Marty B commit suicide—WHY? My answer is I do not know why and 1 don't believe anyone else knows either with the exception of the omniscient, omnipresent, all-powerful—which is GOD. After all, in the final analysis, we're all just God's kids. Obviously!

Ultimately my surrender to Jesus Christ my Lord and Savior not only led me to church every week, I began a Scripture reading and Bible study every morning seven days a week without missing a single day, which will continue for the rest of my life. This in turn led to reading and studying the autobiography of Billy Graham titled *Just as I Am*. In chapter 16, "The Power of the Printed Page," a reference is made to Billy Graham's bestseller, *Peace with God*, published in 1953. I acquired a copy of the book and immersed myself in it immediately. This led listening to Billy Graham's radio broadcast program "Peace with God," which airs every Sunday on the Christian radio station YNOP in Dillon, Montana. YNOP is short for "Your Network of Praise," which my wife and I listen to every day. "I never knew God was all I needed till God was all I had."

I attribute closing quote to Debbie Smith, of High Point, North Carolina.

The Gift of Desperation

In prison with thirty-eight years sober, he hit a whole new bottom. Service was the way out.

Having lived a long life of pretending and trying to look good at all costs, I finally came to the end of my game. At the age of seventy-seven, I was financially, physically, emotionally, and spiritually bankrupt. I had stolen private investors' money; it was unintentional, but I was negligent in my actions. A judge sentenced me to five years for my crime and I entered Four Mile Correctional Center in Canyon City, Colorado.

On that first day of prison, during the intake process, I cried genuine tears. Even though I had thirty-eight years of sobriety behind me, I now found myself locked up. I had reached the final stage of self-will running riot in my head. For the first time in my life, I honestly made an attempt to surrender my life to God. I informed my intake correctional officer that I might kill myself the first chance I got. A mental health counselor then informed me that

---

I had a choice to make: I would someday leave prison and I could leave it bitter, better, or in a box

---

I had a choice to make: I would someday leave prison and I could leave it bitter, better, or in a box. At times it wasn't an easy choice.

I still thought I was smarter than anyone on this ball of dirt. But I recognized that this new world of prison life and its inmates had the power to hurt, maim, or kill. Early one morning in my cell, I decided I wanted to somehow live through this chapter of my life. What was I going to do? In a way, I felt relief; I was exhausted. I definitely knew my old life was over. I realized I no longer had to pretend or try to look good. I remembered I was once told by a friend in

AA (Alcoholics Anonymous) that the last place I needed to show up looking good was an AA meeting. I found out quickly that the same is true in prison.

I was alone and spiritually ill as I entered my new home, a 6' x 8' cell, also known as a closet. I had broken the law and victimized good people. I had pled guilty and been sentenced to five years in prison to be followed by three years of parole, plus $212,000 in restitution to be paid to my victims. This excellent thinking had gotten me to prison and I deserved to be there.

I looked back over my years of sobriety in AA. Was it possible for me to have missed the spiritual message found in the Big Book? Of course it was! I'd lived all those years in spiritual bankruptcy. I'd worked a program for one year and then repeated the same year for thirty-seven years. I thought sobriety would be enough and the rest of the program could be disregarded. How wrong I was. I've heard it said that, "Life is tough. But it's tougher when you're stupid." And it's toughest without a Higher Power.

I realized that at my age, my five-year sentence could be a life sentence. I thought it possible that I could die in prison. Despite all this, my self-centered pride kept telling me it just couldn't end this way. Surely I was destined for something better. So I began my surrender in pursuit of some form of God. What I did not know then was that Four Mile prison would become a new starting point for me—my gift of desperation.

I prison, thanks to AA, I discovered that false pride was undoubtedly my biggest defect of character and that my

---

If I was ever going to know real freedom and true happiness, the price to be paid was the destruction of my self-centeredness and leveling of all my pride

---

lifelong separation from God was my main problem. At long last, I had hit my bottom. Knowing full well that I could not possibly rectify my wrongs, I sought God's guidance and direction. I decided I would make a sincere written amend to each of my victims for my wrongdoing. If I was ever going to know real freedom and true happiness, the price to be paid was the destruction of my self-centeredness and leveling of all my pride. I felt as though God announced his arrival with a wrecking ball and flattened everything in my life. And through it all, I could hear a still, small voice asking, "Are you ready to make a new beginning?"

And I did. I stayed sober and secured a job in the prison system as a GED instructor, helping inmates who could only read at a third- or fourth- grade level. My most unforgettable student was a guy named Michael. I was able to help him get his GED diploma and then later also help him write his parole papers to the prison board of parole. He was paroled after eight years of time served. It was one of the most humbling experiences in my entire life and one that I will never forget.

There are many other prison friends I will never forget as well. Three of them became good friends. They were the most remarkable men I have ever known. They were honest, sincere, and trustworthy. They introduced me to the "upside" of prison life. That's right … I said upside. These men saved my life—behind razor-sharp barbed wire. What a deal I was handed, and it was completely undeserved. It was the beginning of God's gift to me.

Why do we wait so long to surrender

and pray? Why do we waste our God-given life? I actually found a new life, a new freedom, and a new happiness—all while incarcerated.

I used to believe that my character defects were so strong they would probably die thirty minutes after I did. Not anymore.

Capture the Vision

On that day in September 2011, when I was sentenced to five years in the Four Mile Correctional Center in Canyon city, Colorado, I had lost all hope. At the age of seventy-two, this felt like a death sentence, since I could die before my release date. At long last, all by myself and in light of my circumstances, I made the decision to turn my will and my life over to the care of God without any reservations. This is a step I now fully realized I had never completely taken in my previous thirty-eight years of sobriety in Alcoholics Anonymous. I finally realized the life is impossible for me without GOD.

I was justifiably accused and ultimately convicted. Don't misunderstand this statement. I'm not a victim. Prison is one of the best things that ever happened to me on this ball of dirt Let me share something I've learned about prayer in prison, since it's one of the benefits of the upside of prison. That's right I said upside! I call it the prayer of surrender. In prison, beaten and defeated, worn out, I gave up. I admitted for the first time in my life I lost the war. It was over and I felt aloneand peaceful. With my gift of desperation, I became aware of the power in the prayer of surrender. I no

With my gift of desperation, I became aware of the power in the prayer of surrender

longer had to look good or pretend for anyone or anything. I finally ceased fighting for good and all.

In order for me to capture the vision of Alcoholics Anonymous from the upside of prison I would have to unequivocally realize the hardest thing I would ever have to do was to surrender my self- will while knowing that it was the one thing in my life that my Higher Power would never violate. This was pretty heavy stuff. Nevertheless, this is the price I had to pay. I was to learn the four paradoxes of AA: I must surrender to win; I would have to die before I could live; I would have to cry before I could laugh; and I would have to give it away in order to keep it. To be squarely up against the paradox of surrender to win was to become an absolute must for my recovery, freedom, and happiness if I was ever to make a successful return to the mainstream of life with four decades of sobriety. My whole attitude and outlook upon life changed as I was now completely willing to align my will with the will of my Higher Power. I finally realized this was the proper use of the will. He allowed me to capture the vision of AA while serving time in prison.

Prison became God's gift of desperation to me. What should have occurred a long time ago was now obvious and was burned into my consciousness that I could get well regardless of anyone or anything. I had arrived and I ceased fighting everything. I was sick and tired of being sick and tired and decided to give myself a break. I was worn out from pretending, and it was now over. My Higher Power was the only one who knew exactly who I was and why I was in prison. I surrendered all to God and turned my entire attention to the program AA as outlined in the Big Book and to the fellowship I found in prison.

My new identity was now prison inmate #155498. However, my sobriety was permanent for good and all and it was burned into my consciousness that I could get well regardless of anything or anyone. This was the miracle of healing from God as I understood Him. No longer would I live in darkness and fear as a prisoner in my own skin; I was reborn while incarcerated. I now understand about the good, the bad, and the recovered. I was sober all these years by the grace God and the twelve steps

I had to learn that there is some good in bad people and some bad in good people

of Alcoholics Anonymous. As mentioned before, while in prison I landed the best job I had ever had. I became a GED instructor, helping other inmates acquire their GED diploma. I was paid a whopping $10 a month all while experiencing a new freedom and a new happiness through my gift of desperation all wrapped up in humility—what a deal!

Sure, there are a lot of bad people in prison. That's the downside. But, the upside is that there are also a lot of good people who can be trusted and who are caring and honest. As a felon who served all his time at Four Mile prison in Canyon city, Colorado, and now lives with his beautiful wife in Dillon, Montana, I know what it is to be sincere, but I also know I can be sincerely wrong. I realize I know only a little and more will be revealed by God as I understand him. I had to learn that there is some good in bad people and some bad in good people.

"If you think you are an atheist, an agnostic, a skeptic, or have any other form of intellectual pride which keeps you from accepting what is in this book, I feel sorry for you. If you still think you are strong enough to beat the game alone that is your affair. But if you really and truly want to quit drinking liquor for good and all, and sincerely feel that you must have some help, we know that we have an answer for you. It never fails if you go about it with one half the zeal you have been in the habit of showing when you were getting another drink. Your Heavenly Father will never let you down!" This is a direct quote from Dr. Bob Smith, co-founder of AA, in "Dr. Bob's Nightmare," his own personal story found in the *Big Book* of AA.

"Our book is meant to be suggestive only. We realize we know only a little. God will constantly disclose more to you and to us. Ask Him in your morning meditation what you can do each day for the man who is still sick. The answers will come, if your own house is in order. But obviously you cannot transmit something you haven't got. See to it that your relationship with Him is right, and great events will come to pass for you and countless others. This is the great fact for us."

I just quoted two of the most important paragraphs I found in the Big Book of Alcoholics Anonymous. By the grace of God and the principles of Alcoholics Anonymous, I have finally recovered from a seemingly hopeless state of mind and body. I must apply this program to my life daily and carry its vision into all my activities. Since having now been granted the "Keys of the Kingdom," I am now able to share in a general way how it was, what happened, and what it's like now. Although it took four and a half decades, rest assured, it's never too late. The AA program is God's gift to the alcoholic and totally unmerited. For sure it has to be the greatest program for a bunch of drunks and only GOD knew that if ever a group of people needed each other it would be all of us.

LETTERS

April 7, 2014

Hi Maggie,

I hope this card and note finds you healthy, happy, and in good spirits and that it doesn't appear to be in poor taste. I wish only that your life is the very best it can be for you, Jason, your family, and all those who surround you. Quite frankly, however, I have an ulterior motive for contacting you and may it seem like only a small favor or simple request since I really do not know who else to ask and I sincerely believe you'll understand.

Since I am now happily married to Elaine and living in big sky country—the small town of Dillon in southwestern Montana. My backyard is Beaverhead County which has some of the finest fly fishing one could ever hope to find. I finally believe I'm approaching some of the simpler things that life has to offer. I actually feel like I'm living in God's backyard; it's so beautiful.

I hope my simple request is not too much to ask, since Jason and I are estranged and I seek no reconciliation and believe he doesn't either. It's really all okay and I take full responsibility for everything I've done in the past. I made some very poor choices and decisions late in life and "a price had to be paid" in full by me and no other. 4 Mile Prison in Canyon City was exactly what I needed and deserved, and I do not regret one day of my time served. When I entered prison, I left behind some personal things that I now wish I could somehow get back.

Please try to understand that I am not what I should be and I'm not what I want to be but thank God I'm not what I used to be

---

Namely, two black cowboy hats, two western belts, and my buck hunting knife with its black leather sheath. I sure could use these things for my outdoor activities such as fly fishing. If these items are still somehow packed away is there any way you could possibly send them to me? And I would be of course most willing to pay the postage or the cost of shipping. This is my request and if it is not at all possible I assure you I will understand, however, would you please let me know either way?

In closing may I say that I liked you from the very first moment we met before I was sentenced to 4 Mile and permit me to now add I think you are one fine lady and Jason is one fortunate man to be married to you and he most certainly appears to be under God's favor and I don't believe for one second I'm talking out of turn. Please try to understand that I am not what I should be and I'm not what I want to be but thank God I'm not what I used to be. I'm sure with my record it can only be GOD's grace and His divine intervention that I would also meet my very best friend in life while incarcerated in prison. God willing, we will meet again in a year or so when hopefully Adam will be released from prison having been down over fifteen years. He is the most remarkable man I have ever met in my life. Maggie, I wish for you and Jason the best always that this life and beyond has to offer. Myself, I have never been happier and more at peace, so be good to yourself and look always to the "Father of Light" who presides over us all.

Sincerely,

Richard

May 8, 2014

Dad,

I think you pretty much know we no longer have any of your things. By writing to Maggie, I suspect it's your way of trying to let me know, for whatever reason, you are happy and doing well. Of course, I don't believe you, but no matter. I do appreciate that you think very highly of Maggie (right on there—she's the best) and that you wish us well. I honestly wish you well too, but that doesn't mean I'm going to pull any punches about how I feel.

I haven't responded to your most recent cards and letters quite simply because I see no change in you. To me, you are a person who has no capacity to be honest and genuine. With what you have communicated to us, I can't help but find you still delusional, narcissistic, and with a perpetual need to try to save face. You reaching out to Maggie is completely inappropriate, whatever your motivations may be. She really doesn't wish to have any correspondence with you, and we both agreed I should be the one to respond.

You once told me you would make it up to me, concerning the "guaranteed" money I confidently invested with you. I don't suppose your way of making it up to me is by letting me know (through writing to my wife) that you are happily remarried, healthy, and spending your time fly fishing in "God's backyard"? I know your word

---

I give you credit for admitting that, but that doesn't mean everything is okay and you're excused

---

means nothing, and you have written off any idea of making it up to me, whatever that meant. You have owned up to the fact that you have failed in every area of your fife. I give you credit for admitting that, but that doesn't mean everything is okay and you're excused. You say you made mistakes "later" in life. I would say that is quite the miscalculation, and I won't bother to spell it out for you. For someone who has been in AA for over forty years, you seem to have no ability or understanding of how to make amends. If you think you do, you haven't learned anything from AA. Personally, I think really you are just too much of a coward. I remain shocked and amazed AA has been such an important part of your life given who you are. You stated the price for your mistakes has been paid by you and you alone. Wow, you couldn't be more clueless and self-absorbed.

Given that you don't wish to reconcile, and the fact that you must know (per your instructions long ago) we wouldn't be hanging on to your cowboy hat, buck knife, and belts, your letter looks like little more than another lame attempt to somehow redeem yourself. None of us care to hear any of it. You clearly show no ability or desire to redeem yourself in any respectable way. You truly have no further reason to reach out to me. I ask that you don't.

Sincerely,

Jason

November 20, 2014

Jason,

I'm going to be specific and very direct so you'll know exactly how I now feel. "I never knew God was all I needed till God was all I had." One never has to apologize for anything they don't say, however, I have plenty to say and no more apologies will be made. With respect to personal belongings, read your first letter dated November 30, 2011, and my response dated December 3, 2011, and then read your note dated July 30, 2020. The chronology is obvious and self-explanatory. Prior to your letter of July 30, 2012, I wrote to you asking if by chance you might have some of my identification. That was all and in turn you sent me a box containing approximately thirty items with your July 30 note enclosed. The parcel was mailed to me in Craig, Colorado, and inventoried by the CAPS facility before I was granted possession. Some of its contents were cowboy boots, tennis shoes, winter scarfs, raincoat, denim jeans, cellphone, identification cards (Social Security and Medicare), socks, underwear, Navy cap, black leather jacket, polo shirts, two belts, windbreaker jacket, sweat shirt, OAC turtleneck, white and gray turtlenecks, black cowboy boots, denim jacket, rollup blue hat etc. etc. etc., do you get the picture? Now go back and re-read my letter to Maggie dated April 7, 2014. I'll quote from my letter, "I hope my simple request is not too much to ask, since Jason and I are estranged and I seek no reconciliation and believe he doesn't either." This is a true statement, subsequently I ask for "two black cowboy hats, two western belts, and my buck hunting knife with its black leather sheath." The brown western belt buckle encased a 1975 AA international convention medallion which was held at Currigan Hall in Denver, Colorado. This would have value only to me and no one else since I was there with barely two- and one-half years sobriety and you were only five years old.

Your remark about my long-term sobriety in AA certainly exposes how focused you are with your own self-importance. You don't have a clue what you're talking about and I'll tell you why. You have not been on the firing line of AA to see the broken families of practicing alcoholics and the abuse of children. It brings misunderstanding, fierce resentment, financial insecurity, disgusted friends and relatives, warped lives of blameless children, sad wives and parents. It has the demonic capacity to annihilate everything that's worthwhile in life. This type of insanity is a nightmare for everyone involved which

---

It has the demonic capacity to annihilate everything that's worthwhile in life

---

is way beyond belief or comprehension. So much so it's indescribable and the mental and emotional pain is unbearable. Many believe suicide is the only way out. I lost my best friend in AA due to suicide after he had only five years sobriety. In a helpless and hopeless state of mind, suicide looked like a step up from where Martin was at and sadly there are many others like him. I've been to approximately 13,680 AA meetings over the course of my sobriety and I needed every one of them to maintain my freedom from what was once my master, King Alcohol.

Did I always say and do the right thing in AA to help others? Absolutely not. More often than not, I was too self-absorbed to extend a helping hand. However, I will say this, if it wasn't for AA and the grace of God your life growing up would have been a living nightmare without any of the benefits you appeared to enjoy. Jason, don't talk down to me about AA or making an amend. I made my amend in the very first letter I wrote to you. I'll paraphrase since I'll never forget what I said because it was sincerely made from the bowels of my heart. I admitted I was wrong and it was unkind of me. I showed you no respect. I gave you no dignity and I was deeply sorry. I embarrassed you in front of your family, relatives, friends, and of course Maggie and I had no call to do that. Even though I wanted to make a point, I never should have done it. I apologized. If for whatever reason you cannot or will not recall or accept this, fine, but it's not okay—it's just your choice.

There are some wrongs I can never fully right, and this undoubtedly is one of them. I can honestly say I would right it if I could, but obviously I cannot, therefore it's also your choice whether or not to digest this letter. But please stop being such a fool since you have plenty of your own stuff to work on. Your anger should be your first concern, but of course it's your decision. I readily admit after working a good AA program for some fifteen years I still managed to take back the reins and run my life into a ditch and ultimately end up in prison. I now refuse to live in the past and I suggest you get over it, especially since AA is God's turf and not yours.

Perhaps you might recall that during the first century a great Man was brutally beaten and nailed to a cross for all to see. Some of His parting words were, "Father, forgive them, for they know not what they do" (Luke 23:34, KJV). Guess what? Two thousand years later and I still don't know what to do and neither do you. I really pray you get this. Actually, one could say the whole world is still trying to figure out what to do. Less than 3% of the people that enter Alcoholics Anonymous stay sober for the remainder of their life. Sad but true! They exist in a hopeless and helpless state of mind and body. Although I've been allowed to stay sober over forty years, I personally failed to perfect and enlarge a fit spiritual condition which the program demands. Well, that just about covers it AA.

There's so much more I could ask and question and comment on but it's so mundane I really don't want to, and I really don't care to. I'd be remiss if I didn't say I honestly hope your mom and Lisa are okay because I sometimes wonder about them, especially Lisa's drinking and what not. At the risk of your displeasure, Elaine and I will continue to live in "God's backyard," happy, joyous, and free, and very much in love.

In closing, going back again 2,000 years, man decided to challenge the Supreme Being of the universe; they lost and thought they had won. I now find this incredibly arrogant and profoundly stupid. Twenty centuries later there remains only one Book that definitively explains this. It shows the only true way and I've decided to follow it. I hope and pray one day you and Maggie will find it.

Richard

September 15, 2015

Hello David [my brother-in-law],

It was surreal seeing Jim and Barbara at the hardware store in Dillon, Montana. Although our visit was brief, I enjoyed seeing them. They both look very happy and healthy. My wife Elaine and I drove to Wise River, Montana, hoping to give Jim the enclosed card and photos for Lisa.

Needless to say, we were unable to locate Jim and therefore, I'm sending them to you along with a simple request.

I reflect every day upon my present blessings

Would you please give these to Lisa if it is convenient? And I thank you in advance. If this is not possible please kindly return them to me.

Since my time in prison, and my life now with Elaine, I "reflect every day upon my present blessings—of which every man has many—not on my past misfortunes of which all men have some"

(Charles Dickens, *A Christmas Carol and Other Christmas Writings*).
Sincerely,

Richard

Conclusion

"There is a principle which is a bar against all information, and which cannot fail to keep a man in everlasting ignorance-that principle is contempt prior to investigation" (Herbert Spencer).

After four trips through the Holy Bible from cover to cover, I'm convinced I know only a little and more will be revealed as I continue without excuse. The Spirit-filled life is neither a theory nor hyperbole— I choose to live it. Being the good, the bad, and the forgiven, I still fall far short of the goal.

Will I receive an offer I can't refuse? In the words of the beautiful song by MercyMe, I CAN ONLY IMAGINE.

TEACH Services, Inc.
P U B L I S H I N G

We invite you to view the complete
selection of titles we publish at:
www.TEACHServices.com

We encourage you to write us
with your thoughts about this,
or any other book we publish at:
info@TEACHServices.com

TEACH Services' titles may be purchased in
bulk quantities for educational, fund-raising,
business, or promotional use.
bulksales@TEACHServices.com

Finally, if you are interested in seeing
your own book in print, please contact us at:
publishing@TEACHServices.com
We are happy to review your manuscript at no charge.

www.ingramcontent.com/pod-product-compliance
Lightning Source LLC
Chambersburg PA
CBHW071751090426
42738CB00011B/2647